YOU Be YOU!

The Kid's Guide to Gender, Sexuality, and Family

Jonathan Branfman

Illustrated by Julie Benbassat

Jessica Kingsley Publishers
London and Philadelphia

Dear Parents, Guardians, and Educators,

Welcome to **You Be You!**

This book makes gender identity, romantic orientation, and family diversity easy to explain to kids. We also cover discrimination, privilege, and how to stand up for what's right. Our aim is to help raise kids who accept themselves and others.

This book is for children aged 5 and up, and it's split into short sections that build on each other. Read a little or a bunch at a time—whatever you and your kids feel like.

Enjoy, and help build a happier, more accepting world!

Warmly,

Jon & Julie

Part by Part

1 Getting Started

People have lots of funny ideas about boys, girls, and love! Like maybe you've heard the idea that everyone has to be a boy or a girl.

And that every boy will grow up to be a man, and fall in love with a woman. And that every girl will grow up to be a woman, and fall in love with a man.

And maybe you've heard that everyone who falls in love has to get married...

...and that everyone who gets married has to have children.

And maybe you've heard that all boys should like
the color blue and play sports and wear pants. And
that only girls should like pink and play with dolls
and wear dresses.

Well, surprise! These ideas aren't true. And that's great news.

Every person is different, and that's what we call diversity. This diversity is a beautiful thing!

 2 The Sexes

Maybe you've heard that there are two sexes, male and female. When you're born, the doctor assigns you a sex based on what body parts you have. If you have a penis and testes, you're called male, and if you have a vagina, clitoris, and ovaries, you're called female.

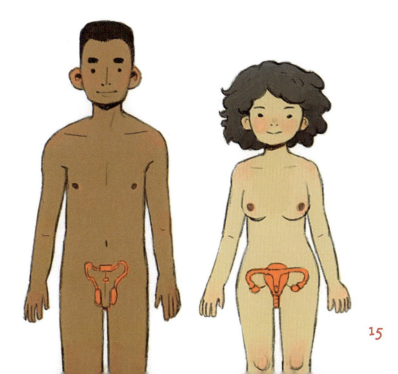

These body parts are shaped by the chromosomes you inherit from your parents. Chromosomes are like building guides. They're inside every cell of your body, and they tell your body how to grow. The X and Y chromosomes decide what sex parts you'll have. Most people with XY chromosomes have male parts, and most people with XX chromosomes have female parts.

But actually, not everyone is born with a body that fits these expectations of male or female. Some people have a mix of male and female parts, like a vagina and testes. Some people with XY chromosomes have female parts, and some people with XX chromosomes have male parts. Some people also have XXX or XXY chromosomes.

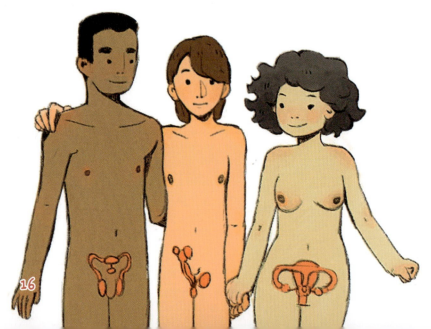

People who aren't male or female are called intersex.
And being intersex, male, or female are all great!

Just like the world has tons of different colors,
not just blue and pink, people's bodies come in
all different types. And just like every color is
beautiful and good, so is every type of body.

3 Gender

Sex is how people name bodies with different parts.
Gender is how people expect those bodies to act.

For example, some people expect a female person to
like pink dresses, and expect a male person to like
playing football.

These expectations are called stereotypes. Stereotypes are when you think you know all about a person just by how they look, where they live, or how they speak. For example, assuming that you know how smart someone is, what they're good at, and what they like to do for fun.

But actually, stereotypes are silly! No matter what kind of body you have, you can like any type of color, clothing, food, or activity.

So no matter what body parts you have, you can wear blue and pink and yellow and green, and anything else! And you can like football and dolls and swimming and anything you think is fun!

Gender **identity** is how you see yourself as a boy, a girl, or any other gender.

Maybe you've heard that every male person must see himself as a boy or a man, and that every female person must see herself as a girl or a woman.

But guess what? That's not so. A person's sex (what kind of body they have) doesn't decide their gender identity (how they see themselves).

So whether you have a male body, a female body, or an intersex body, you might see yourself as a boy, a girl, or a different gender, like genderqueer or gender non-binary. And that's fine!

If your gender identity matches the sex you were assigned at birth, you're called cisgender. For example, if you were assigned female and you identify as a girl, you're a cisgender girl.

If your gender identity doesn't match the sex you were assigned at birth, you're called transgender. For example, if you were assigned male at birth and identify as a girl, you're a transgender girl.

And some people don't identify as either boys
or girls. Many people who feel this way identify
as gender non-binary, genderqueer, gender
nonconforming, or genderfluid.

And being cisgender, transgender, genderqueer, and gender nonconforming are all great!

Some transgender and genderqueer people want
to change their bodies, to look more like the
gender they identify with. This change is called
transitioning. People transition by going to
the doctor for special medicine called hormone
treatment, and sometimes also for surgery.

But some transgender or genderqueer people don't
want to transition, or just want to transition by
changing their clothes or hair, and that's fine too!
And some people would like to transition, but don't
have money to pay for it.

And no matter your gender identity, and no matter how your body looks, you can wear any colors and clothes you want, and do any activities you want, and have long or short hair, or both! You be you!

When people grow up, many feel romantically attracted to some other people. Attraction can feel like you really want to spend time with that person, or ask them on a date, or hold their hand, or kiss them.

Many people start to feel romantic attractions around age 11 or 12, but some start feeling attraction at younger or older ages.

Some people don't ever feel this kind of romantic attraction, and that's perfectly okay. People who feel this way are called asexual or aromantic.

Some asexual people do have romantic emotional relationships, but don't feel interested in physical actions like kissing.

For people who do feel romantic attractions, some are attracted to only one gender, and some are attracted to more than one.

Some people feel romantically attracted to people of their own gender, like a man who's attracted to other men, or a woman who's attracted to other women.

People who are attracted to their own gender are called gay. Some people also say "homosexual," but this word is outdated. Women who are attracted to other women are also called lesbians.

Some people are attracted to a different gender,
like men who are attracted to women, or women
who are attracted to men. People who feel this way
are called straight or heterosexual.

Some people are attracted to more than one gender. For example, a man who is attracted to men, women, and genderqueer people. People who feel this way are called bisexual or pansexual.

All these different types of attraction are called "orientations," "romantic orientations," or "sexual orientations." Any person with any kind of body and any gender identity can have any kind of sexual orientation.

For example, an intersex person who identifies as a woman could be attracted to men, women, genderqueer people, all, or none. Same for a cisgender man, a transgender woman, or anyone else.

And no matter what genders you feel attracted to or not, that's totally fine!

Sometimes when you feel attracted to someone, and they feel attracted to you, and you've known each other well for a long time, you fall in love.

Romantic love is when people are attracted to each other, and care very much about each other, and like spending lots of time together, and probably also like kissing each other.

Sometimes when people fall in love, they get married. But not everyone chooses to get married, and that's perfectly okay. Marriage is a personal choice for you and the person you love.

If and when you decide to get married, or not get married, your choice is totally great.

6 Having Kids

Maybe you've heard that everyone who gets married has to have children, and that only married people can have children.

Well, real life is a lot more complex and diverse, and that's okay!

Some people who get married want children very much. This can be true for cisgender or transgender or genderqueer people, for straight or gay or bisexual or asexual people.

These people can all be great parents and raise happy, healthy children.

But not everyone who gets married wants to have children, and that's fine too! Sometimes people know for sure that they don't want to have children, and sometimes people just want to wait a while before they have children. When you grow up, whatever you want is okay!

Some people also have children without being married, and this is also okay! Unmarried couples, and single people of any gender or orientation, can be great parents who raise happy and healthy children.

The big idea is: No matter what kind of body you have, and no matter who you're attracted to, and no matter whether you're married or not, it's entirely up to you whether you want to have kids. And whatever you choose is great!

7 Discrimination

Stereotypes about sex, gender, and romantic orientation lead to **discrimination**. Discrimination is when someone says mean things to you, or hurts you, or limits your options in life, because of some trait you have. Discrimination is **always** wrong.

There are many kinds of discrimination, like discrimination based on your skin color, your gender, your sexual orientation, whether you have a disability, where you're from, or how much money you earn.

Lots of people face many kinds of discrimination at once.

Discrimination based on sex is called **sexism**. Some people think that folks who identify as girls or women are weaker and less intelligent than folks who identify as boys and men.

In the past, because of these sexist ideas, women weren't allowed to vote, own property, or work in well-paying jobs! And even though these laws have changed, you may still meet people who think this way.

Discrimination based on gender identity is called **transphobia**. Transphobia is when a person doesn't like you just for being genderqueer or transgender.

Genderqueer and transgender people face a lot of bullying because of transphobia. Some intersex people also face transphobia if they don't fit expectations for how boys and girls "should" look. Sometimes transphobic bullying even comes from the police and the government!

For example, in some American states there are laws blocking genderqueer, transgender, and intersex people from using the bathroom of the gender they identify with. This makes life very hard when you just have to pee.

Discrimination based on sexual orientation is called **homophobia**. Homophobia is when people are mean to someone just for being gay, lesbian, bisexual, pansexual, or asexual.

Like transphobia, homophobia can include mean words, physical harm, and legal discrimination.

For example, until recently, many states in the USA prevented two women or two men from marrying, and from adopting children.

In some American states, it's still legal to fire someone from their job or kick them out of their house for being gay, lesbian, bisexual, pansexual, or asexual. Plus, in some schools, teachers can be fired just for saying that it's okay to be gay, and okay to be transgender.

Discrimination specifically against bisexual or pansexual people is called biphobia. For example, some people still don't believe it's possible to feel attracted to more than one gender, and tell bisexual people that they're just making things up. How silly!

All these forms of discrimination are always wrong. Facing discrimination can make you feel very sad or angry or both. And those feelings are totally okay.

But whenever you're facing discrimination and feeling bad, remember that there are lots of good people in the world who will support you and help you! And remember, it's always your responsibility to help other people, too!

8 Privilege

When people discriminate against you, it's easy to notice. It can be harder to notice the opposite— when people treat you nicely because of some trait you can't control, like being male or cisgender or heterosexual.

The opposite of **discrimination** is **privilege**. Privilege is when you get advantages, or nice treatment, or an easier life just because of who you are.

Many people don't notice their privileges, even when they use those privileges every day. For example, if you're cisgender, think about the last time you had to pee. You probably never worried about whether other people would let you enter the bathroom, or if the police would come to stop you from peeing.

But transgender people have to worry about this problem all the time! So if you can go to the bathroom without worrying, and without getting in trouble with the police, that's an example of privilege: Your life is easier because you're cisgender.

Another example is men's privilege. People often assume that men are smarter, stronger, and better leaders than women. So even when women say or do the same things, men often get more respect, more money from their job, and better promotions.

Having privilege doesn't mean you never have any problems, or that your life is always easy. It means there are some specific problems you don't face that other people around you face all the time.

And it's so important to **notice** those problems, even when they don't happen to you personally! For example, this man is sad because he spilled his coffee, but he should still notice that he's earning more than women at his job who do the same work.

Having privilege also doesn't mean you're a bad person. It just means you need to keep a few things in mind. First, when you succeed at school or work, don't assume it's **only** because you're smarter and better than other people.

And don't assume that other people are failing just because they're dumber or lazier.

Remember, you might be doing better than other people because life is putting less trouble in your path. And other people might be doing worse because they face discrimination you don't.

Second, if you see a chance to use your privilege to help other people, help them! We'll talk more about how to help others a little later.

9 Intersectionality

Everybody has lots of identities at once. Like you might be an able-bodied Latina Muslim lesbian cisgender girl, a white bisexual genderqueer Christian person with autism, a black Jewish straight cisgender boy with deafness, and so on.

Because everyone has lots of identities, most people face many kinds of discrimination **and** many privileges at the same time. This is called **intersectionality**.

For example, if you're a gay boy, people might treat you badly for being gay (that's **homophobia**), but also treat you better than girls (that's **male privilege**).

Or if you're a white transgender girl, people might treat you nicely for being white (that's **white privilege**), but also disrespect you for being a girl (that's **sexism**) and for being transgender (that's **transphobia**), all at the same time.

In order to understand how people are treating us, and also to understand what others around us are experiencing, we need to think about this intersectionality.

 10 Being an Ally

An ally is someone who stands up against discrimination, even discrimination that doesn't hurt them personally. So basically, an ally uses their **privilege** to support people facing **discrimination**.

For example, an ally can be a straight person who helps gay people fight homophobia.

An ally can also be a cisgender person who helps genderqueer and transgender people fight transphobia.

And an ally can be a cisgender or transgender man who helps women fight against sexism.

How do you be an ally? Well, first, make sure you never say or do anything mean to anybody, or about anybody, just because they're different from you in some way.

Second, listen to what other people say about their own life experiences, and believe them. For example, if you're a boy, you might be very surprised to hear what problems girls and women face from sexism.

You might feel so surprised that it's hard at first to believe them—but remember, they're the ones who are facing sexism first-hand! So they know, and you should learn from them.

The same thing goes if you're a straight person listening to gay, lesbian, bisexual, pansexual, and asexual people, or a cisgender person listening to transgender people.

Third, if you hear or see discrimination, do something about it! For example, if you hear classmates tell mean jokes about gay people, or see them insulting a woman, or see them hitting a transgender person...

...tell a teacher or your parents! And you can even tell the mean people to stop, if it's safe for you to talk to them. You can also go up to the person they were hurting, and say kind, supportive things.

11 You Be You!

So remember, there are many kinds of people in the world, and this diversity is a good thing! No matter what kind of body you have, and no matter what gender you identify with, and no matter who you're attracted to, that's great! And whether you want to get married or not, and want to have kids or not, that's wonderful too!

And whenever you meet someone who's different from you, you should always be nice to them, and help them fight discrimination.

You be you! And help others be themselves.

The End

Who Made This Book Possible?

You Be You! helps kids to access decades' worth of wisdom from social justice-minded activists and academics. Many people first come across these ideas at age 18 in university classes, which is very late in the game. Plus, attending university is still an opportunity that many people never experience.

We believe the world can be a kinder place if more of us start learning these social justice ideas as children—if these ideas become as familiar as fairytales and nursery rhymes.

To that end, this book conveys ideas from many, many feminist, LGBTQIA, and anti-racist thinkers, especially women and LGBTQIA people of color. For adults reading this, we highly encourage you to check out their work!

A few of the most influential thinkers who've inspired this book include: Ella Shohat, Loolwa Khazzoum, Melanie Kaye/Kantrowitz, Marla Brettschneider, Evelyn Torton Beck, Irena Klepfisz, Kimberlé Crenshaw, Audre Lorde, Barbara Smith, Barbara Christian, Cherríe Moraga, Gloria Anzaldúa, Angela Davis, María Lugones, Betty Friedan, Jewel Gomez, Peggy McIntosh, Gayatri Spivak, Mia McKenzie, Janani Balasubramanian, Alok Vaid-Menon, Urvashi Vaid, John D'Emilio, George Chauncey, Sylvia Rivera, Daniel Halperin, Judith Butler, Marilyn Frye, Michael Messner, Donald Sabo, Harry Brod, Paula Hymen, Karen Brodkin Sachs, Daniel Boyarin, Jonathan Boyarin, Eric Goldstein, and Matthew Frye Jacobson.

We are deeply indebted to these authors, and all the others who have helped to create the ideas that this book presents for children. We hope that *You Be You* honors their vision, and helps to create the kinder society they have imagined.

Meet the Author

Jonathan Branfman

Jon grew up in New Jersey, and is pursuing an academic career in Gender Studies. He loves working with kids, and enjoyed seven exhausting-but-unbeatable summers as a camp counselor. Jon now continues his love for teaching at the Ohio State University, where he completed his PhD in 2019. Combining his summer camp and university experiences, Jon created *You Be You* to help kids understand gender, romantic, and family diversity from an early age.

At OSU, Jon's research topic is Jewish masculinity in pop culture (think of Drake, Adam Sandler, and Amy Schumer). He teaches classes on gender, sexuality, and race in the media more generally. Jon's interests also include gender and sexuality in Jewish theology, and Jewish LGBTQIA inclusion.

Jon thanks his family, friends, and OSU colleagues for their wonderful support on this project and so much more. In Columbus, special thanks to Sara Rodríguez-Argüelles Riva, Nick Painter, Rachel Richman, Liz and Jordan Berman, and Philip and Malia Womack. Jon also thanks Julie for bringing this book to life with her beautiful art, and thanks Andrew James at Jessica Kingsley Publishers for guiding it to press.

Meet the Illustrator

Julie Benbassat

Julie is a current student at the Rhode Island School of Design, pursuing a BFA in illustration. She enjoys drinking tea, listening to wholesome podcasts, and going on nature walks. When she is not studying or freelancing, she is known to be reading botany books or drawing outside.

Reflecting on her own experiences, as well as those of her friends from high school and college, helped Julie to illustrate the images in *You Be You*. Her goal is to help kids see and value the diversity in love, gender, race, and family structure.

of related interest

Who Are You?
The Kid's Guide to Gender Identity
Brook Pessin-Whedbee
Illustrated by Naomi Bardoff
ISBN 978 1 78592 728 7
eISBN 978 1 78450 580 6

Phoenix Goes to School
A Story to Support Transgender and Gender Diverse Children
Michelle and Phoenix Finch
Illustrated by Sharon Davey
ISBN 978 1 78592 821 5
eISBN 978 1 78450 924 8

A House for Everyone
A Story to Help Children Learn about Gender Identity and Gender Expression
Jo Hirst
Illustrated by Naomi Bardoff
ISBN 978 1 78592 448 4
eISBN 978 1 78450 823 4

All You Need Is Love
Celebrating Families of All Shapes and Sizes
Shanni Collins
ISBN 978 1 78592 251 0
eISBN 978 1 78450 534 9

Vincent the Vixen
A Story to Help Children Learn about Gender Identity
Alice Reeves
Illustrated by Phoebe Kirk
ISBN 978 1 78592 450 7
eISBN 978 1 78450 826 5

The Prince and the Frog
A Story to Help Children Learn about Same-Sex Relationships
Olly Pike
ISBN 978 1 78592 382 1
eISBN 978 1 78450 731 2

First published in 2019
by Jessica Kingsley Publishers
73 Collier Street
London N1 9BE, UK
and
400 Market Street, Suite 400
Philadelphia, PA 19106, USA

www.jkp.com

Library of Congress Cataloging in Publication Data
A CIP catalog record for this book is available from the Library of Congress

British Library Cataloguing in Publication Data
A CIP catalogue record for this book is available from the British Library

ISBN 978 1 78775 010 4
eISBN 978 1 78775 011 1

Printed and bound in China